# THE GIFT -
# A REVOLUTION
# IN NETWORKING
# MASTERY

MATTHEW FERRY, THACH NGUYEN
MARC SACHNOFF & KRISTEN MARIE SCHUERLEIN

The Gift — A Revolution in Networking Mastery
by Matthew Ferry, Thach Nguyen, Marc Sachnoff
and Kristen Marie Schuerlein

First Edition, 2012

Published by Global Rakkaus Press

Art Design: Tiane Loredo

Printed in USA

# Table of Contents

# Why We Wrote This, and What's in it for You

Are you ready to experience more results from your networking and sales efforts?

Are you having trouble making networking "work" for you?

Are you a natural connector who feels isolated?

Are you wondering where the switch is to open the floodgates of referrals you know are there?

If so, we bet you're wondering why networking isn't really working. We imagine that you're tired of putting in the time it takes to network but getting little in return.

It's time for a new paradigm.

Are you ready?

We want to personally show you how to revolutionize your networking. No selling, no self-promoting, no hidden agendas. Just authentic conversation, genuine interest and incredible connections that will impact your bottom line and the rest of your life.

For many people, traditional networking just isn't happening. On the surface, it is the friendly exchange of the elevator pitch. Underneath, you may feel that it is about pressuring strangers to do something they may not want to do, like buy your product or service.

Sure, we all want to create results, but how we approach networking—what we say, do and how we follow up—can be the difference between endless struggling and consistently building our business. It can be the difference between getting the life sucked out of us or feeling exhilarated, excited and fulfilled.

This book is our personal invitation for you to join us in experiencing a totally new approach to networking.

A revolution has begun.

And you can be part of it.

# Welcome to the Revolution

We live in uncertain times. You may be feeling confused, like the rules have changed but no one gave you the new handbook. We know the feeling.

The four of us have been through amazing ups and downs over the last several years, and we want to share with you our discoveries and how they can help you navigate today's business climate. We want you to prosper, to make money and to experience happiness and joy while doing it.

Each of us has had major business and personal setbacks. Three of us crashed businesses, leaving a trail of financial wreckage to clean up. One of us is in the midst of getting square with the IRS. One had to sell a prized Rolls Royce, the symbol of years of hard work. Another had to sell a home. And one ended a long-term relationship, discovered the office had been robbed and no longer had a place to live—all within 24 hours.

So we know times are tough.

But we've found a way to punch through the darkness and paralysis. As a result, we've refined a process that's guaranteed to generate results in your life. We'll give you the step-by-step process that we used to turn our businesses and our lives around in amazing ways.

We want to introduce you to something timeless, yet extraordinarily in tune with today's world and its challenges. It's something that has forever changed all of our lives. It's not a religion, but it is a powerful life philosophy that anyone of any age can use right now. It's not a self-help routine, it's not positive thinking, and it's not a scam. It's a revolution, but there are no armies to defeat, just a new set of tools and ways of thinking that can literally change everything.

Because everything we do involves interacting with others, we've chosen networking as the stage to display these principles. It is through actively networking, meeting people, in groups and one on one, that we discovered how powerful The Gift is.

Everything worth doing requires effort. That includes The Gift. Yet it's also fun and will power up your business, your relationships and your life in ways you might never have thought possible. Using these principles now will help move you through whatever you're facing as well as lay the foundation for incredible growth in the years to come.

In short, your life will never be the same.

We have come to believe every person can live a life of...

- Unlimited Abundance, Prosperity and Freedom

- Limitless Possibility, Inspiration and Purpose

- Boundless Hope, Trust and Faith

- Deep Connectedness, Belonging and Community

- Incredible Joy, Happiness and Fulfillment

It may sound impossible to you now. We simply ask that you approach this with an open mind and open heart, because some of it will seem counter-intuitive.

*Just go with us and see what happens...*

*To your success and happiness,*
*Matthew, Thach, Marc and Kristen*

Co-Founders, The Gift
January 2012

# Networking as We Know It

## An Empowering Journey

People have been networking since, well, since there have been people. The ancient marketplace, the teahouses, the inns and village squares, anywhere people gathered naturally led to a sharing of ideas, news, gossip and the promotion of goods and services.

Networking can be an extremely powerful way to grow your business. Where else can you come together with a group of professionals who are committed to success? Where else can you surround yourself with others who want to grow? Where else can you build relationships with like-minded folks who enjoy what they do?

Nowadays, many business people seek opportunities for

face-to-face networking because they believe that there's the potential for higher quality relationships when people meet and interact in person vs. online or over email. And most of us lean toward these kinds of face-to-face interactions because people tend to prefer actually knowing and meeting the people with whom they're considering doing business.

When it comes to networking, there are typically two ends of the spectrum—"I am really lousy at this and I hate it!" or "I am a really great networker." Most folks find themselves somewhere in between.

Regardless of our level of experience, at some point we all ask ourselves:

- *Am I doing this right?*

- *Why do I feel awkward when I network?*

- *What if I don't get enough business?*

- *How can I make a good impression so people will refer business to me?*

- *Why am I not getting the results I see others getting?*

Don't worry — whether new to networking or a seasoned pro, you are about to begin an empowering journey that is sure to have profound results in your business and in your life.

"But," you insist, "I'm already networking. So why aren't I getting results? Is it the process, or is it me?"

> Have you ever felt traditional networking is about pressuring strangers to do something they may not want to do, like buy your product or service?

Consider the illusion that we've all bought into: that if you do this well, you will get more business out of this group, these individuals, and finally, you will prosper.

But it doesn't really work that way. And, deep down, you know it.

## Traditional Networking Doesn't Work

Have you ever felt like traditional networking is about pressuring strangers to do something they may not want to do, like buy your product or service? Has it ever felt like a forced environment of polite assaults that invariably ends with stilted interactions?

Can you imagine leaving a networking event enlivened and excited, having made a difference for others and others having made a difference for you? What if you could be a magnet in your networking group? What if you didn't have to work the room? What if people and business just seemed to flow to you? What if all you had to do was contribute to others in a natural way and have everything you want in your business and in your life come to you?

*Giving The Gift opens your world to all kinds of new possibilities that are surprising and delightful. I've got an intention to make a movie, and this side project is written down as a commitment, but it's not something I'm totally focused on.*

I got invited to a dinner and a hockey game. It was an unusual event because I didn't know anybody. In fact, I didn't even know the host. But my friend was invited to this event, and he couldn't go, and he suggested to the host to invite me, that I would be an interesting character to come along.

I accepted the invitation, and when I showed up at dinner I walked into a room with eighteen people I didn't know. I sat down at dinner, and I felt completely comfortable. This is not normal for me to feel completely comfortable, but it has become normal now because I give The Gift. There's no pressure on me to perform or look good or be smart or witty or funny. All I have to do is find out about other people, find out what they're about, where they're going, what they're doing, what they're up to in their life, and see if I can make a difference and contribute to them. It makes life so easy, because I don't have to think about me and how I look.

I immediately started giving The Gift to the people around me. It turned out that one gentleman to whom I was giving The Gift had just completed his own movie. How could I have known?

As we were talking, I was looking for ways to contribute while discovering ways that I could help and support him. Naturally he wanted to turn it back around: "Tell me about what you're doing." I said, "I found it so interesting that you had just done a movie. I'm doing a movie as a side project." We began talking about it, and low and behold, that relationship has turned into a key relationship that has accelerated the process of my movie. At the time of this writing, I am still relishing in the delight of this serendipitous and most amazing connection that I made. That is the power of giving The Gift, you'll find yourself in the right place at the right time all the time.

THE
GIFT

Chapter 2

# Time for a Networking Revolution

## Runners, Take Your Mark

If you are like us, you are aiming to experience extraordinary results. Getting a referral that turns into a valuable business feels great! You love being in the zone. Having business opportunities seem to fall into your lap and watching your business grow with a life of its own.

What if you could do exactly what you are doing and increase your results?

What if you could walk into any networking group, any environment and be a magnet for connections, ideas and success?

What if you were free of lack, fear or concern in your business and your life?

What if you were successful no matter who was in the room?

What if you could effortlessly tap into the true potential and promise of networking?

Our vision is to inspire you to experience what is possible when you change your approach to networking. When you start with the goal to be of the highest service to others, everyone gets what they want. It's fun. It's rewarding. And it works.

> What if you were free of lack, fear or concern in your business and your life?

This is what the four of us have discovered. And our lives have been transformed. It's a race in which everyone wins. This is what The Gift is all about.

*One of my favorite things is to jump on the phone and call through my database. I particularly love to talk to people I don't see much or don't know well. It's a powerful way to shift my focus from my worries and concerns by simply being interested in other people. I will never forget the day I called Ann-Marie. We'd been introduced a couple years earlier, but our paths had crossed only occasionally.*

*Before I made this call, I was feeling anxious, knowing I needed to close some business in the coming week. Part of my brain said, "What are you doing, just calling people? You need to get into sales mode, sister!" But I stayed true to my commitment to call people for the pure joy of discovering what is happening in their world.*

*After the usual greetings, I used the Discovery Process [see Chapter 8] to dive a little deeper into the conversation. I wanted Ann-Marie to know I was genuinely interested in her, in her life and in going beyond small talk.*

*On this day, it turns out that Ann-Marie really needed to connect with another business owner. As the call went on, I decided to completely release the nagging "I have to close some business" voice in my head. Thank goodness I did. I became a sounding board for Ann-Marie—to listen, to share and to be a trusted confidante as she talked through a significant challenge she was facing in her business.*

That conversation changed her life and mine. That was the day our friendship blossomed. I left the call grateful that I could be so authentically present for another person, and she apparently left the call inspired and with a new perspective. How do I know? She called the next day to thank me for contributing my time and energy so fully to her and her business, without any expectation.

Ann-Marie and I have built a deep trust and appreciation for one another personally and professionally. Additionally, Ann-Marie has hired my company to work for her company, all while becoming an outstanding referral partner.

Do all calls go like this? No. Did I expect anything out of or in return for the time she and I spent on the phone that day? Certainly not. But what I do know is that taking the time to really meet someone at the level of that person's need, in that moment, is a powerful way to run your life and your business.

The punch line: Contributing to others is simple when you remove yourself and your needs from the equation.

And what's even better: You never know when or how you can make a difference for others when you just trust that you can.

# Chapter 3

# What is The Gift?

## In The Shoes Of Another

What you're about to learn is a practical, elegantly simple process that opens the doors for your business goals and personal dreams to be fulfilled.

You know what it feels like to find the perfect birthday gift —when you see the delight on someone's face and you know that they know that what you're giving is exactly what they want. It isn't about what you wanted to give them. It's about what they truly wanted to receive. That is the essence and the power of The Gift.

It's about standing in the shoes of another and helping that person get what he or she wants.

Think back to when you were a kid. You didn't have any

trouble telling your parents, grandparents and friends what you wanted for your birthday. If they were listening (and could afford it), your birthday brought you exactly what you wanted. Remember the excitement, the delight and the butterflies you felt knowing that others wanted to give you exactly what you wanted to receive?

Now, imagine being known as someone who creates that experience for others all the time, and in the process receives exactly what you need when you need it.

The Gift boils down to a simple prescription: To get everything you want in your life and business, all you have to do is help others get what they want.

## The Law Of Contribution

The Gift is based on the Law of Contribution, which states *that the level of your happiness and success is directly proportional to the number of people you serve selflessly.*

How do we know it's a Law? Because it works time after time. And we didn't just make it up.

King Solomon knew it.

Buddha knew it.

Confucius knew it.

Aristotle knew it.

*"One man gives freely, yet grows all the richer; another with-holds what he should give, and only suffers want."* — Proverbs 11:24

*"When you see someone who is practicing giving, aid him joyfully, and you will obtain vast and great blessings."* — Buddha, The Sutra of Forty-two Sections

*"To be able to practice five things everywhere under heaven constitutes perfect virtue.... [They are] gravity, generosity of soul, sincerity, earnestness, and kindness." — Confucius, The Analects*

*"The greatest virtues are those which are most useful to other persons." — Aristotle*

## Why Give The Gift?

Imagine when you have dozens, hundreds or even thousands of people supporting your business. Your life will never be the same again. Everything you need will start coming to you with ease.

By giving The Gift, you will achieve extraordinary results:

1. You will experience the emotional high of contributing to others without expecting anything in return.

2. You will become someone whose goals and dreams materialize automatically as a function of the incredible good will that you create in the world.

3. You will create a powerful group of advocates, believers, supporters and followers who assist you in building your business.

Simply put, we believe anything is possible when you connect deeply with others.

And there's no better place to start experiencing the

> To get everything you want in your life and business, all you have to do is help others get what they want.

power of The Gift than at networking events, group meetings and industry cocktail parties—anywhere that business people gather.

This is an ongoing process... a life long attitude... a permanent shift.. that accelerates the more intentional it is.... and the more consistently it is activated.

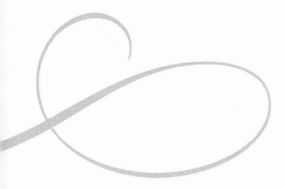

# Chapter 4

# The Gift Process

## Connecting The Dots

By now you're wondering, "How the heck do I get started with this Gift thing?"

It's easy, and you can begin right now. The Gift is an elegantly simple, yet profound four-step process.

1. Connect deeply with others.

2. Find out what they need right now.

3. Contribute on the spot.

4. Watch miracles occur in your life.

# Connect Deeply With Others

There are two essential aspects to this first step:

- Be interested in others.

- Every person you meet is important.

Essentially, all you have to do is get interested in others. Be curious about their business or life. Ask questions (we'll give you some to consider in a later chapter). Talk about *them*, not you.

The cool thing about connecting deeply with others is that the moment you become interested in someone else, it becomes impossible for you to worry about yourself or your business. Feeling awkward and being curious about others cannot exist at the same time. Doesn't it sound great to be free—even for a few minutes—from the grinding pressure of your own problems?

Next, consider this: Every person you meet has the potential to contribute to your deepest desires. As you discover that this is true, you realize that stepping over people slows down the speed at which your goals come true. It's easy to decide that someone isn't worth your time—we all do it. But we've learned through The Gift that the person right in front of you could be the messenger carrying the solution you've been looking for.

Especially when networking, trust that you are in the right place at the right time to meet the right people. You have no idea who will be the right person with the right information or the right connection. When you take the time to connect deeply with others, all of your intentions will manifest. That's why we say, "Step over no one; contribute to everyone."

## Find Out What They Need Right Now

Really understanding what others need is a big idea. Discover what will help them move forward on an important project, idea or problem. What are they missing? What could be a solution? Here is where you can dive deeper than the standard small talk that pervades typical networking exchanges.

## Contribute On the Spot

This is where the fun begins. Turn on your creativity and compassion. Offer ideas, advice, connections, support, whatever might help get where they want to go. The more you understand what another is seeking, the larger the contribution you can make.

You may not think you have anything to give to others. You may not know their business, their industry or have any idea how their company runs. Don't worry. If you've really been listening—listening with a heart of service—then ideas, thoughts, connections and introductions will naturally come to mind. There's a reason for this (which we'll talk about in a later chapter), because when you are in a state of contribution, you are literally in a state of grace. And in such a state, something will come to you that may surprise even you.

If you can't think of anything to give, know that just listening and acknowledging what others want is important—it is, is in fact a gift.

It's about being mindful and intentional.

> The more you contribute to others, the more others naturally want to contribute to you.

## Watch Miracles Occur In Your Life

Ready? The more you contribute to others, the more others naturally want to contribute to you. When we talk about miracles, we are talking about "unexpected good fortune." It could come from someone to whom you have directly contributed, or it might come from someone you don't know or a source you didn't expect.

In fact, the results you're seeking could come right out of the blue, left field, or from someone you'd never have imagined could assist you in accomplishing your goal. We experience this all the time in giving The Gift, but we never cease to be amazed by how the universe delivers.

How cool is that?!

## Don't Believe Us

Try this little experiment yourself. Pick a day when you have two meetings to attend. Before you go into the first meeting, take a moment to ask yourself, "What's in it for me?" Put on your observer glasses and watch how this meeting goes with your what's-in-it-for-me mind frame.

Then, before you go into the second meeting, ask yourself, "In this meeting, how can I add value to others?" See what happens and how it's different from your first meeting.

That's why we say that *The Gift is an enlightened process.*

Take the first step...

Experience the joy...

Take the next step...

And experience even more joy...

## KRISTEN'S STORY - *A Constant Adventure*

*Upon leaving a networking event, I started chatting with a woman. I got super curious about her, and quickly we discovered that we knew several people in common. It was one of those "Wow, I can't believe we never met before this" moments. As we continued talking, she told me she was ready to embark on a new career. She shared her passion and gave me an idea of what she was looking for. I took her card and made myself a note. In total, we spent less than 10 minutes together.*

*Fast forward a month. I am on a list-serve with a host of business owners who share job openings. It takes me about 2 minutes to read it daily and think about the people I know who would be a fit for the positions available. Bingo. I found a job listing perfect for my new acquaintance, so I jumped on the phone to get permission to send along this opportunity.*

*I think she was a little blown away that I'd remembered our conversation, and that I took the time to help in her quest for a new job. I sent the email, and to my delight she called me back in about an hour— she had an interview the next day!*

*The excitement and appreciation in her voice made my day. What a joy to help others and see them light up when they move toward their dreams.*

*I felt like a million bucks getting to contribute to her in this way. Giving The Gift daily makes life fun, interesting, joyous and a constant adventure!*

# Chapter 5

# The Paradox of Giving

## An Absolute Truth

The Gift is about allowing yourself to give and receive all the goodies that the universe has in store for you. Many people are really good at receiving but lousy at giving. Our culture has encouraged a whole generation of "takers" who believe that happiness and success come when you grab all you can get. Takers believe that there's a limited amount of fortune or stuff, and if they don't grab it, someone else will.

But that hasn't proven to be the ticket to fulfillment.

We believe the world is one of unlimited abundance, so scarcity is not an issue when you give The Gift.

Likewise, there are folks who are natural givers—they give, give, give. They are kind and considerate people. But when you try to give to *them*, they close up tighter than a clam. They just can't seem to receive, to embrace and accept the gifts that others want to give them.

Neither of these approaches by themselves is the key to experiencing the joy and benefit of a contributive life. And a contributive life is the way to attract incredible success in business.

So herein lies what we call the Paradox of Giving:

You must give in order to receive, and...

You must receive in order to give.

We have learned through years of hard effort, setbacks, challenges, frustrations and disappointments that the Law of Contribution is a two-way street.

This is an absolute truth.

> You must give in order to receive, and...You must receive in order to give. 🙶

Our goal is to teach you to become boundless, agenda-free contributors and, at the same time, limitless, grateful receivers. When we can give without agenda and receive without hesitation, the universe opens up, and connections, business, money, relationships all flow naturally. This is what some people call *being in the zone.*

In order to engage the magic of The Gift, *receive what is offered, listen to advice with an open mind, and follow up on potential leads.*

Here's another part of the Paradox of Giving: When we are facing our most difficult, desperate moment, that is exactly when we need to give The Gift. That's right, the times when we might feel compelled to focus only on ourselves and our crises are the perfect times to employ The Gift by giving to others, without inserting our own agenda (hidden or overt).

We all know people who are stuck on this one. They have big problems, issues or obstacles and are constantly reminding us about them and pressing us to help them. Their problems seem urgent, but what they don't realize is that their actions are like trying to attract flies with vinegar. And so, they get the opposite response, and in turn they become even more desperate. They unintentionally repel those who might help. Thus, the cycle continues.

*That's why we believe that giving or contributing to others in a way that is meaningful to them is the key to break through any obstacle, deadlock or breakdown.*

A friend who has been with us on this journey to create and clarify The Gift once told us that when she is in authentic, full-on connection and contribution with another person, she feels like she is in a state of grace.

Wouldn't you rather feel like you were in a state of grace instead of the gnawing desperation that comes from feeling powerless over your challenges and problems? That's why The Gift and its Law of Contribution are so powerful.

A final thought about giving and receiving: One pitfall you might experience when beginning The Gift process is *expecting* people to reciprocate and then being disappointed when they don't. The Gift is not based on the idea of one-to-one reciprocity. Just because you contribute to Bernie Businessman does not mean that Bernie will contribute to you. You intentionally contribute—that is, make a difference—for whoever is right in front of you. As a result, you open yourself up to receiving and allow the Law of Contribution to work its magic. In doing so, you give up your agenda about who is supposed to contribute to you and how that person should contribute.

*Not long ago, I moved to Seattle after many years in Los Angeles. Not knowing many people in town, a new friend invited me to a technology industry association mixer at a local brewery. Armed with a desire to be of service without agenda, I happily threw myself into the crowd. I was simply giving The Gift in whatever way I could to everyone I met, even if only for a brief moment or two. My friend introduced me to someone who was in the fitness industry, and we exchanged cards.*

*Now, I have learned to always follow up with people I meet, so I sent this person an email telling him that I enjoyed meeting him. About a month later, I got an email back from him, inviting me to meet to talk about a major new initiative in the company. I agreed to meet, this time in line with my "one hour rule," which means I'm willing to give any sincere person The Gift for an hour. Where it might lead, I leave to the universe to sort out.*

*Well, that meeting was an eye-opener. Much to my surprise, the company was creating a new digital network, an area in which I have some expertise. They had looked at my website, read about The Gift and my goal to "Bring the Buddha to Business." The long and short of it is that they hired me to consult with them as they launched their network. This person has become a great client and source of business.*

*So, you never know where the benefits of The Gift will come from. They could come literally from "out of the blue" or, in this case, cyberspace.*

Chapter 6

# The Gift: What it Is and What it Isn't

## Think You Know? Think Again

Consider that giving The Gift—choosing to contribute to others—takes intention and mindfulness. From our years of refining The Gift, here are some distinctions we'd like to share with you about what contribution is and what it's not.

CONTRIBUTION IS:

- Once you have enough information, offering a valuable resource.

- Introducing or referring people you believe will be helpful (see the section on Advocacy in Chapter 8).

- Telling others about a service that you know and trust.

> ....contribution is about giving up your agenda and simply contributing to others, no strings attached. **"**

- Providing information that will move the person forward.

- With permission, coaching or brainstorming together.

- Supporting or helping in a way that is uplifting to all involved.

- Listening attentively and expressing support for the person's goal, even if you cannot help with something specific.

Remember, acknowledgment is a contribution to us all.

CONTRIBUTION IS NOT:

- Asking "How can I help you?" Instead, use The Discovery Process (see Chapter 8).

- Selling your product or service. That's not contributing, that's just sales.

- Giving your product or service as an unstated bribe to get the other person to give you something of theirs.

- Putting yourself at risk. If you are willing to put yourself at risk to contribute, then you might want to ask yourself if you believe there is something to gain that is of greater value than the risk you are taking.

- Making promises you can't keep. Consider that if you make a promise you know you won't or can't keep, you are being deceptive. Deception is the antithesis of contribution.

- Trying to look good to the person to whom you are contributing. Wanting to look good is all about you and not about the needs of the person to whom you are trying to contribute.

In a nutshell, contribution is about giving up your agenda and simply contributing to others, no strings attached. If there are any strings attached, it ain't contribution, it's just cleverly disguised manipulation.

A final thought about what contribution is and isn't. Sometimes people desperately want to contribute, but they don't take the time to listen. They jump to conclusions after a moment or two and assume they know what's best for the person in front of them. This is not authentic contribution. When people try to contribute without fully listening to someone, they only succeed in being annoying, because others can tell they haven't listened. Rather than making a genuine contribution, these people have an agenda to look good, be smart or win another person's favor. But it eventually backfires and repels people. So listen carefully before offering any contribution.

# Chapter 7

# Do-Be-Do-Be-Do

## "Doing" and "Being"

One of the great things about being part of a formal networking group is the structure they create to encourage connections and referrals. Many times there is a system or a process that is core to the group. This is the secret sauce that makes the group unique.

The focus tends to be what we call "doing," or the action part of networking: giving your elevator pitch, exchanging cards, making presentations, offering referrals to others. All good.

We propose you continue "'doing'" these things. We also propose you consider who you are "'being'" in the process.

It's who you are "being" when you are "doing" that makes you successful at networking and in life. Look at it like this:

Highly successful athletes combine "doing" and "being" to win the gold. The "doing" is the action; the "being" is the mindset.

In choosing to experience all The Gift has to offer, we ask that you...

**BE willing to explore a new way.** Hey, if you already had the answer you wouldn't be reading this book. So be willing to think outside the box.

**BE willing to release that you know how your dreams will manifest.** We sometimes think we know the best way to accomplish our goals. But when you start giving The Gift, you may discover that you are naturally discovering a better, easier or more valuable path.

**BE willing to be interested in others for the pure joy of it.** If you can suspend your judgment of the person in front of you and simply put your attention on what he or she needs, you will find relief from your own troubles, and the stuff that bubbles up out of your life will not only help them, it will make you feel great, too.

**BE open to trusting that you are in the right place at the right time.** Most people are oblivious to others around them except when they need something from them or are annoyed by them. But everyone in our environment is there for a reason. We have something to give them, and they have something to share with us. It's up to you to discover what that is.

So the next time you attend a formal networking event, take a moment beforehand to consciously and intentionally put yourself in what we call a state of contribution: be ready to stand

> It's who you are "being" when you are "doing" that makes you successful at networking and in life.

in the shoes of another and discover how you can make a difference in someone's life. Check out the appendix for some of our favorite intentions.

It's not every day that you get to meet a billionaire. At least, not for me.

When I moved to Seattle, a friend invited me to a charity event that was being hosted by a billionaire. I learned that this person was passionate about a certain movement for social change—a passion I happened to share. Before the dinner began, my friend introduced me to this person and I mentioned our common interest. This launched our host on a 20-minute conversation about this issue, to the exclusion of all the other arriving guests. I told him that I would be happy to read his proposal for a new organization to help solve this issue, and he agreed to send it to me.

A few days later, an email arrived with the proposal, which I read with interest. I wrote comments and suggestions and sent them back.

Now, keep in mind, I had just arrived in town —I had no job and little regular income at the time. And here I was, connecting with a person with unlimited means. It took a lot of fortitude and a deep understanding of the Law of Contribution to keep from hitting him up for help.

We met a couple of times, and he found my suggestions valuable. At one meeting, he revealed that, despite a large organization around him, he was the only person pushing this project forward. He looked at me and asked me if I would be interested in running this new organization. As I had just moved to town *and didn't know the players in what was already an emotionally charged environment, I politely demurred.*

*But my new friend understood immediately, and he made two powerful and unexpected offers: 1) He would hire me to rewrite the business plan with him and to assist him in getting the organization off the ground, and 2) He would help me by making introductions to potential employers on my behalf. Believe me, the effect of these introductions by a person of his level in the community had enormous influence and continues to impact my life in a positive way.*

*So, giving The Gift without an agenda isn't easy. But by keeping to the pureness of being of service to others, amazing things happen. And they continue to happen in my life.*

# Chapter 8

# Mastering The Gift

## Who Do You Have To Become ?

Choosing to be someone who naturally contributes to others is vital to mastering The Gift. Essentially, you are making the choice to become someone who discovers who people are and what they are committed to, and then contribute to them in a positive way. This is the way to master true contribution in any networking event.

There are three aspects to learning The Gift that will forever transform your networking experience:

**1. Become a person who is interested in other people.**
You might be thinking, "But most people are boring, and I have nothing in common with them." That perception keeps you from moving your business forward. When you choose

to be interested in everyone you meet, your goals and dreams materialize at rapid speed.

The Universe/God/Source Energy is trying to deliver your goals and dreams to you in the fastest possible way. Often the right information comes to you from people you never would have expected it from. Being interested opens you up to meeting new people and connecting with people you would have never dealt with in the past. This creates the possibility for rapid expansion in your life.

**2. Listen for what people need in order to take a next step toward their goal.** As you seek to master The Gift, you start to listen for what people really need right now. The questions in The Discovery Process help give you a window into what's going on in their business and life. This is the first step in developing a clear understanding of how you can contribute right now. Continue to ask questions until how you might contribute becomes clear.

**3. Contribute without an agenda.** This is a crucial skill in The Gift. When you give for the sake of helping that person, your life will accelerate and expand in ways that you cannot currently imagine. When you contribute without an agenda, you put yourself into a state of "no need." For people in a state of "no need," everything comes to them seemingly effortlessly, because *when you are fulfilled, you attract more of what fulfills you.*

Formal networking events are the perfect arena for mastering The Gift. Regardless of where others are at in their perception of networking, simply give The Gift and see what happens.

# Becoming Magnetic

The more you practice The Gift, the more you will see how easy it is to make things happen in your business and your life. Have you ever watched people at an event who were literally magnetic? Others are naturally drawn to them. Their energy, their reputation and how they are perceived by others are undeniable.

Those same qualities can be yours.

> Imagine having legions of supporters, followers, believers and advocates interested in you. "

Imagine being known as someone who is interested in others. Imagine drawing to you all the people, resources and ideas you need to move your business forward without pushing, coercing or manipulating. Imagine having legions of supporters, followers, believers and advocates interested in you. *This all possible when you shift your perspective from "what can you do for me?" to "how can I be of service to you right now?"*

# Advocacy—Harnessing The Power Of People

An Advocate is a person who connects those who can benefit from knowing one another. We all know someone who is a connector. They just love introducing the right people to you at the right time. It's like they're thinking about your needs even when you're not around. That's the Advocate in action.

Through The Discovery Process, this person collects information about how to contribute to others in the future. The Advocate knows the difference advocacy makes in his or her own life, and takes contribution seriously. It's almost like the Advocate carries a mental checklist of the wants and needs of others and uses that to create opportunities that make a difference.

As an Advocate, you are constantly looking for ways to help the people you have met by finding and introducing resources, ideas and people to help them get what they want. Intentionally choosing to advocate means you are committed to expanding your own network by expanding other people's networks. The more people you know, the more access you have to the resources you need to build your business and profit from your efforts.

Here's a juicy secret for you: Do this, and over time you will become a person who builds a cadre of people who willingly advocate for you. With an army of advocates, what you desire shows up easily and effortlessly.

Choosing to be an Advocate for others simply accelerates your life.

## The Discovery Process

There are three ways you can start conversations with people. Simply ask:

1. What is one of your business goals?

2. What are you excited about in your life right now?

3. What are you committed to?

Use The Discovery Process to help further clarify how you can contribute.

- Tell me more about that.

- Help me understand what you mean.

- How will that benefit you?

- What are you trying to accomplish by doing that?

- What's important about that to you?

- How will that move you forward?

Complete your conversation with this:

- What do you need right now to get on the path and make that happen?

- If I were to tell other people about what you are looking for, what would I say?

## THACH'S STORY - *Advocating For Scoutreach*

*I sit on the board of Scoutreach, a division of the Boy Scouts that emphasizes service to minority groups, and they are always looking for ways to raise money for the Boy Scouts. Since I sit on the board, I always have my eyes and ears open to advocate for them.*

*Recently, I was having lunch with the manager of a downtown bank branch. I began asking about his business, how he's doing in today's economic climate, who is his perfect client, and how he goes about getting more clients.*

*Business was great, he told me. In fact, his branch was the only one to break even within two years after opening. To build his clientele, he said he organized* cool events, like renting out Safeco Field or a boat on Lake Washington or a ballroom to host parties to thank their existing clients and also invite new people.

"I know the owner of a luxury car dealership," I said. "What would you think about throwing a cool event arranging for your clients to drive something sporty around a race track?"

"Let's do it!" he said. "If you can set that up, I would appreciate it so much."

The owner of the luxury car dealership appreciated the connection and so did the bank.

The branch manager thanked me afterward, and asked, "What can I help you with?"

I told him about Scoutreach and what its mission is.

He got excited and asked how he could help. When I told him they were looking for sponsors for their annual fundraiser, he agreed without hesitation. Scoutreach was so appreciative and grateful.

# Mastering Introductions Is Key to Building Deep Relationships

Have you ever been at an event where someone came up to you and said something like: "I've been looking all over for you; I want you to meet Bob. You guys have a lot in common." Even if you hate meeting new people, there's no easier way than to have someone else do all the heavy lifting. Funny thing is, it's much easier to introduce one person to another than it is to meet people yourself. And usually both parties now hold you in higher esteem for having made the effort to make the introduction.

But like everything we do in The Gift, introductions must be handled with clear intentions based on the spirit of contribution, or they can backfire on you. Here are three suggested guidelines for making introductions based on The Gift.

**1. Don't make an introduction until you get a good sense of who this new person is.** If you do not follow The Discovery Process, you cannot authentically contribute to your new friend or your current network. In other words, don't put your friends in compromising positions by introducing them to new people about whom you know little.

**2. Respect the wishes of your friends and associates.** In other words, don't introduce new people to them unless you have their permission to do so. For example: we have friends in the movie business. If we don't get their permission before making introductions, it can be seen as imposing on them, and we risk losing them as friends.

**3. Don't misrepresent your relationship with this new person to others.** When you make introductions, make it clear that you just met and that you only suspect there might be something valuable in their meeting. Leave it up to the two of them to discover if there really is synergy.

# Introductions As Contribution

Introductions are valuable to others when they are win/win. One objective in The Gift is to create introductions that will be mutually beneficial for your new acquaintance and your current network of friends. Maybe you've experienced this: an email pops in your inbox with a "Hey, you HAVE to meet this person." No explanation. No request. Just a demand on your time and attention. Consider that random introductions without properly qualifying them will reflect badly on you. No one needs another thing to do. Everyone appreciates a thoughtful introduction that helps move ahead whatever they are working on right now.

The point is to contribute to both the new person and your current network in a way that creates real win/win situations for everyone.

A final thought about introductions: It's perfectly OK to let a meeting with someone new ripen a bit before introducing that person to one of your contacts or friends. We think you'll find that the better you know the people you are introducing, the better the introduction will go. Go with your gut and do what feels right.

One of the greatest benefits of The Gift is never being alone. What do we mean? So many of us feel alone, because we don't have enough people to help us achieve our daily tasks, big goals, and ultimate dreams.

When you embrace The Gift process, you will never be alone.

When you have a network of Advocates, Supporters, Believers and Followers who are committed to helping you get everything you want, your life will be dramatically different.

The more you give The Gift as a natural part of your daily actions, the more people, one by one will naturally become your Advocates, Supporters, Believers and Followers. It's like having a deep bench, a full team, ready to hit the field for any project, challenge or opportunity you need help with!

## Following Up

Masters of The Gift are rigorous about following up and doing what they say they are going to do. Nothing kills the magic that The Gift creates in your life like empty promises and unfulfilled commitments.

We've all experienced meeting someone who promises to support us or help someone we know and then doesn't deliver. Or, they say what they think other people want to hear and then don't follow through.

If you tell someone that you will introduce him or her to a contact, then it is 100 percent your responsibility to do it. That's because, in The Gift, everything we say we'll do is a commitment.

You shouldn't need a reminder call or email from the other party who is waiting for you to fulfill your promise. In a sense, your foremost commitment is to yourself, your determination about the kind of person you want to be in the world. Following up then becomes a natural part of living out who you are.

Your network of Advocates and Supporters will grow to the extent that you follow through on what you commit to. If you earn a reputation as someone who is true to his or her word, your network will grow quickly.

# Chapter 9

# Bringing The Gift to Every Aspect of Your Life

## The Gift Doesn't Just Work For Business

Now that you've opened up to the possibility that contributing to others might work in your business life, it's a natural jump to see the possibilities across the entire spectrum of your life.

## Relationships

How many families never really talk about what's important to each person, let alone find someone around the dinner table who's willing to listen? Getting interested in your family members, finding out what's important to them and contributing on the spot will change the dynamics of your whole family. Imagine having this kind of dialogue with your children, your nieces and nephews, uncles and aunts? Even your own parents?

We know from experience that contributing to those closest to us can be the hardest. For many of us, it's much easier to connect deeply with strangers or business associates than our partners or kids or, heaven forbid, crazy Uncle Al who never lets you get a word in edgewise anyway.

But imagine the possibility of a family in which each person is truly listened to without judgment. Being heard at the dinner table? Now that's a revolution. And as much as we may think we know what's best for our kids (and, yes, we usually do know what's right for them), if we don't give them the experience of being truly heard and warmly contributed to, then how can we expect them to grow up to become natural contributors and receivers themselves?

For one night, or even one hour, just try giving The Gift at family dinner. Connect deeply, find out what they need right now, and contribute on the spot, without an agenda. We guarantee you'll see the beginning of something completely new—a humanistic revolution at home.

## Co-Workers

If you can open the door to a contributive environment at home, just imagine what it might be like to give The Gift to your co-workers. Many workplaces are fun and collaborative spaces where creative work gets done. But most aren't. Most workplaces nowadays are filled with overworked folks who are afraid of saying or doing the wrong thing that might get them canned. This leads to close-mindedness and territorialism that bogs down companies and makes it harder for them to grow.

So one morning, you decide that you will contribute to

everyone you encounter in the office, from the boss to the lowliest go-fer. You connect deeply to each by becoming interested in what they're up to. You find out what they need right now and then contribute on the spot. It could be an idea, a vendor suggestion, a contact, a resource, whatever. Then, without expecting anything in return, just move on to the next person throughout your day. We're not talking about spending an hour with each person; these interactions may last just a few minutes, but can make a real difference in our work relationships.

Funny thing is that when we set up our day to contribute to others, we actually get more done ourselves. Seriously, it may seem counterintuitive, but why listen to us? Try it out for yourself. Remember, we're not saying you should shirk you responsibilities and avoid deadlines or other commitments. We are simply suggesting that you have an alternative to the traditional "If you can't help me get this done, then at least stay out of my way" mentality that pervades modern business.

> ...when we set up our day to contribute to others, we actually get more done ourselves.

## Clients

Clients are the most important player in our business world. Without them, frankly, we'd have no business. So many businesspeople ping pong back and forth between sucking up to clients or trying to get them to do what we want. Both are thinly veiled forms of manipulation. And unless you have a bulletproof monopoly in your market, these tactics are not very effective. Dealing with clients in this manner is tiring, life sapping and not sustainable as a business model.

What if you simply contributed, sincerely and without agenda, and sought to make a difference to each of your clients. In other words, get interested in them as people as well as clients. No, we're not just talking about sending gifts and birthday cards. We're talking about discovering what's happening beyond the scope of your working relationship with them and uncovering how you can contribute in that part of their life.

"Wait a minute," you might be thinking. "What do I care about what's happening outside of why they hired me. Shouldn't I just be focusing on delivering the best product or service possible?" Of course. We agree that you've got to provide great products and services, but contribution masters know that by adding this element of contributing without an agenda, the relationship deepens and doors open. Who knows? You might just have the solution to that problem that's been bugging them, and when you provide it, you are suddenly seen in a new light.

## Everyday Interactions

In sharing The Gift with others, we often tell people, "Step over no one." How many times have we literally stepped over people without even thinking about them?

What would your day be like if you contributed to everyone you encountered in some way or another? Including the people you normally ignore—the waiter in the restaurant, the old man at the newsstand, the cop on the corner, the taxi driver, the flight attendant, the beggar on the street....

In reality, contribution is not a networking tool, it's a way of life. And a life based on contributing to others is the richest life there is on this planet. It's the key to accomplishing your business goals. It's the key to creating a happy, loving family. And it's the key to establishing a life of meaning, of joy and fulfillment.

*Good advice saves millions!*

*In 2006 I was involved in building my dream project, a 251 unit condo development in downtown Seattle. The cost was around $50 million and in order to make this project work I needed to raise $7.3 million – a lot of money!*

*So I went to about 20 of my friends and family members and I promised them I will have the project built and closed by the end of 2008. I also promised them that they would get a very good return on their money. So many of them joined me and invested in the project.*

*We broke ground in the beginning of 2006 and sold out all 251 units within a week. I was so relieved. Now we just had to finish the building and close all the sales by the end of 2008.*

*In the middle of 2008 the real estate market took one of the worst turns in decades and our buyers started backing out one after another. Within a month or so we went from 251 pending sales to literally zero and to make it worse our loan was expiring at the end of 2008.*

*Fear kicked in and I started thinking that if this project goes into foreclosure I will lose everything financially and all my friends and family will lose all their money too. I knew I couldn't let that happen and I had to do whatever it would take to save this project.*

After many days of fear, then mediation, then more stress, we had an inspiring idea to convert this condo project to rental apartments and that way save the deal and all the investors' money.

So we spent all 2009 and 2010 renting the building with the intention that when we got it all leased up the bank would give us permanent financing.

At the end of 2010 we had the building up to 98% occupancy and we went to the bank with high hopes. But instead, they gave us the worst possible news. They said they not only were they not going to give us the permanent financing we needed, but they also wanted us to put the apartment building up for sale and have it sold in 2 months -- otherwise they will file foreclosure on us!

I felt angry, betrayed, and it was so hard to keep on going. But I couldn't stop now because I felt we had come so far and to lose the building was crazy. I told my investors that I would bring their money home and I wanted to keep that promise.

I was paralyzed with fear. My friend Debra asked me, "Thach, what are you resisting?"

"Resisting?" I told her, I'm resisting losing my building, my reputation and all my money!"

She told me that if I had fear as my dominant vibration, if I'm afraid of losing everything and starting over with zero and having to call every investor and tell them the bad news, then I couldn't break through.

Even if I lost everything, she asked me, everything I worked for, would I really be starting over? "You're not accounting for all the resources, the maturity, the knowledge, the smarts, the network you've built up. So even if you became dead broke, you're not really starting over from scratch."

That little talk gave me confidence; it helped me make peace with where I was so I could work through the worst case scenario. I felt the weight lift off me and for the first time in over a year I felt I could create a new vision.

That was the big turning point.

We put the building on the market and within a month we received 11 offers! We took one that was good and all cash and we closed the deal within the time frame that the bank had given us.

It was amazing! Everyone got their money back. I didn't' go bankrupt or lose my reputation. All because my friend contributed to me in my time of need without any goal but to be of service. Now that's contribution!

# Our Big Vision

## Greater Than the Sum of Its Parts

Our mission is to create a world where people naturally
contribute to one another, knowing that when we are in
service to others, we transform our own lives and the
world around us. At our core, we believe anything is
possible when we connect deeply with others.

As the four of us have been refining The Gift, we've
witnessed remarkable results using the principles, process
and philosophy in this book. And we know the same will
be true for you.

Like dropping a pebble in a pond, the ripples created are
infinite, immeasurable and can touch the shores far, far away.
The Gift is the same. One action has the power to create

> One action has the power to create unknown good fortune and impact an untold number of lives. *"*

unknown good fortune and impact an untold number of lives.

As a businessperson, your success, prosperity and well-being make a difference in the world. Join us in giving The Gift. By creating your own network of Advocates, Believers, Supporters and Followers and sharing The Gift, you will ultimately help others do the same.

## MATTHEW'S STORY - *Rising From The Ashes*

*In 2007, my sales training business crumbled around me, partly because of the economy and, of course, my ineffectiveness in managing and understanding how to run a big business. At the end of 2007, I found myself wondering what I was going to do. How did I want to conduct my life and my business now?*

*I made the decision that I did not want a big company any longer; that I wanted a virtual company that would give me the freedom to do whatever I wanted to do, whenever I wanted to do it, and have an unlimited amount of cash flow available. It sounded great, but I had no idea how to actually do that.*

*I had an unusual and interesting request come in. My buddy, Thach—about whom you have been reading in this book, and reading his words as well—called* me up and said a marketing company whose products we had been enjoying as well as doing some training for was planning a trip. Their management team was going to Maui and wanted to do a brainstorming session on how they could do more business by bringing together a group of high-profile people. So they invited me, and they also invited Mark Victor Hansen, James Skinner and Royce Kruger—all well-known figures in the personal growth industry. Mark and James and Royce had all invested in this company, so they had a vested interest, and I was really the only true outsider coming. It was an unusual invitation, and so I said yes.

When I got to Hawaii, I made the decision that I was only going to give The Gift, because the truth was, I was a bit nervous. You know, Mark Victor Hansen, co-creator of the Chicken Soup For The Soul book series, is one of the most successful people in my industry, certainly an icon in the industry of personal development, and I was a little concerned: "Am I good enough? Is he going to think that I'm just a small fish?"

So I made the decision to forget all about that and just give The Gift, and that's it. When I showed up to the meeting, I was in a calm peaceful state, because I wasn't worried about how I looked; I was only focused on finding out what other people were up to. What were they trying to accomplish? Where were they going? How could I contribute? How could I support?

I just dove in, full force, asking questions, being interested, looking for ways that I could contribute and support without any agenda whatsoever. I wasn't *looking for ways in which I could benefit, I was only looking for ways that I could benefit others.*

*Well, the magic was amazing. I ended up connecting with Mark Victor Hansen in a way that I could not possibly have imagined. As we rode home from the meeting together, we both made a commitment in that moment that I would help him to deepen his level of spirituality and spiritual connection, and he would help me to build a million-dollar-a-year business from home that is making a difference for people all across the planet.*

*It was an incredible opportunity to be mentored by someone who had built an empire in my industry, and it all came about by simply giving The Gift.*

# Chapter 11

# Your Next Step

## Change Your Life In Thirty Days Or Less

Are you ready to experience The Gift in your business and your life?

Ready for a challenge? Here are some ideas for putting The Gift into action in your daily life.

## Seven-Day Challenge

Try giving The Gift to someone every single day for seven days straight. Write down your experience or even keep a journal as you give and receive The Gift.

## Fourteen-Day Challenge

Now up the ante and commit to giving The Gift to someone every day for fourteen days. This time, try contributing to people with whom you wouldn't normally interact, people who look different than you, from different cultures, ages or interests. Again, use common sense and don't put yourself in harm's way. But you'll be amazed by what happens when you break out of your comfort zone.

## Thirty-Day Challenge

> ...commit to giving The Gift to someone every day... 〞

If you really want to revolutionize your life, commit to giving The Gift to each person you meet for thirty days. Remember, step over no one. Interactions can be brief; you'll know whether you're connecting or not. This one can really shift deep stuff in your life.

Consider that "networking" isn't just about a group of people in a room. Networking is about connecting. And The Gift is about connecting in a way that helps others, not just yourself.

# Review of The Gift Process

## The Gift's Four-step Process is Easy

1. Connect deeply with others.

2. Find out what they need right now.

3. Contribute on the spot

4. Watch miracles occur in your life.

## The Law of Contribution

Your level of happiness and success is directly proportional to the number of people you serve selflessly.

# Thirty Days of The Gift

Some people like a little assistance in getting started on a new process or goal. With that in mind, here are thirty short reminders about how to give The Gift and the power of doing it consistently. You can read one a day or just circle or copy your favorites.

#1    The Gift is about being of the greatest service to each and every person you come in contact with.

#2    The more you give, the more you will receive. So be ready to have your goals materialize with ease.

#3    Once you become clear about your goal, you can completely forget about it. Just go contribute to others.

#4     When you give, give, give to others… people are going to give, give, give to you.

#5     When connecting with others, try asking, "What are your goals and dreams?"

       "What are you trying to accomplish?"

       "How can I contribute to you?"

#6     The magic of The Gift is that your goals and dreams happen easily and effortlessly when you stop trying to force them to happen and just make a difference for others.

#7     Just give The Gift and watch how the Law of Contribution naturally takes care of the rest.

#8     Stop trying to make the sale and just be there for people.

#9     Intentionally connect deeply with total strangers; find out who they are and what their goals and aspirations are.

#10    The key to giving The Gift to everyone, everywhere, all the time, is to be curious about who they are and what they are up to in their life and their business.

#11    Rather than try to manipulate people to do what you want, find out all about them, be interested in them, discover their goals and dreams and then just contribute.

#12    So many sales people ask clients, "How can I help you?" Instead, find out how you can be of service to them right now.

#13  Discovering who someone is and what he or she
     is committed to is a contribution in and of itself.

#14  "To light a lamp for others will also brighten your own
     way." —Buddha

#15  Listen deeply, because most people feel totally isolated,
     misunderstood and not listened to. Listening is a gift
     in itself.

#16  Often the greatest contribution you can make is the
     authentic, genuine desire to understand fully what
     someone is committed to accomplishing and why.

#17  The Gift leads to clarity, which is attractive and
     reveals next steps, which leads to inspired action.

#18  When you ask a ton of questions, when you are
     concerned about other people's goals and dreams,
     your goals and dreams come faster.

#19  When you are totally interested in people, they get
     totally interested in YOU! That's the best way to have
     tons of Advocates, Supporters, Believers, Followers.

#20  Be curious and ask questions about others. You not
     only appear to be a very wise and important person,
     you become one.

#21  Contribute to someone today on the spot.
     Do something that makes a difference for them.

#22  Serve and give with no agenda. Just trust that all is
     well, and that what you want is coming.

#23    Give The Gift by making a meaningful
introduction today.

#24    Give without expectation of receiving and watch how
fast your own goals are achieved.

#25    By giving The Gift, you begin to create the four
most powerful elements of total success in life:
Advocates, Supporters, Believers, Followers.

#26    You are getting back what you are putting out.

#27    When you have Advocates, Supporters, Believers,
Followers, you simply state your desire to your
network and what you want naturally comes to you.

#28    When you give The Gift daily, get ready to have your
dreams materialize with ease and grace.

#29    The more Advocates, Supporters, Believers, Followers
you have, the easier it is to accomplish your goals
and dreams.

#30    Give The Gift and watch miracles unfold in your life.

# Bring The Gift Crew to Your People

## Let us Give You the Gift

If what you've learned in this book has been helpful to you, then you might want to consider bringing The Gift Crew to your group, company or organization. We are committed to sharing this life-changing process with thousands of people around the country. We create a safe environment where people with no experience with contribution can experience giving and receiving The Gift. These events are exciting, fun and transformational. The results will be better communication, more unity and expanded business results.

If you'd like to learn more about inspiring your organization to greater success, contact us at info@givethegifttoday.com.

And for updates, inspiration and to share your own stories

> Experience giving
> and receiving
> The Gift

visit our website www. GiveTheGiftToday.com

The time has come for a change in the way we do business, to move from a culture of greed to a culture of service. By giving and receiving The Gift, you are on the vanguard of this change. Your company, your industry, the planet and future generations are all waiting for people to step forward into this new paradigm. You've made it this far, now see what unfolds when you put The Gift into action in your life.

And let us know what happens.

*"To light a lamp for another will also brighten your own way."*
*—Buddha*

THE
GIFT

# Acknowledgments and Appreciation

The authors would like to thank all of the people who have helped us develop The Gift into what it is today. The Contribution Networking Party participants, the Power of Contribution groups and many others who devoted countless hours to experimenting with The Gift in events large and small in Seattle, Los Angeles and other parts of the country.

The invaluable feedback from these gatherings brought us countless insights that have helped refine The Gift process into the elegantly simple method you will find presented in this book.

Without the help of so many giving people both in person and online, we could never have completed this work. We have been inspired and encouraged by the many amazing stories that have been shared with us by people who have embraced The Gift in their own lives. We are full of gratitude and appreciation for everyone who has contributed.

## Matthew Ferry

I would like to thank my mentors Mike Ferry, Stuart Wilde, Wayne Dyer, Deepak Chopra, Esther Hicks, David Hawkins & Steven Sadlier. All of whom had a hand in teaching me something that contributed to the ideas in this book.

## Thach Nguyen

I would like to thank my wife Camie and my two sons Russell and Hudson for being on this journey with me. My friends and family for always being there for support, encouragement and inspiration. I would like to dedicate this first book to my dad for being an inspiration and for being an example of contribution in his life.

## Marc Sachnoff

I offer thanks to my wife for her unending support, gratitude to my mother and father for their love, curiosity and passion, and appreciation to my teacher, Dr. Daisaku Ikeda, whose work has inspired me to make the impossible, possible.

## Kristen Marie Schuerlein

I would like to thank those who finds themselves curious about The Gift, have experimented with it, and who ultimately experienced first hand miracles that happen when we consistently apply these principles in daily living.

# About Us

## Matthew Ferry

Matthew is not your typical trainer. He is wild, fun, in your face and a catalyst for profound transformation for thousands of people, just like you, worldwide. He has been coaching, training and inspiring top performing people since 1993. His more then 8300 personal coaching clients include leaders in business... from global executives at esteemed companies like Goldman Sachs to cutting-edge entrepreneurs and sales people who were all seeking to breakthrough what had been stopping them from achieving happiness and success.

## Thach Nguyen

As a realtor, developer and philanthropist Thach hopes to inspire and empower billions of people to reach for their dreams by sharing his life story and showing them that anything is possible. A Vietnamese refugee who once lived in a homeless shelter, Nguyen became a real estate agent with Windermere Real Estate in 1991. Through his legendary determination and persistent door knocking, he became one of Washington state's top real estate producers. Nguyen later joined John L. Scott Real Estate where he sold more than 130 homes a year. He became a millionaire at age 27, three years ahead of his aggressive schedule. Today, he and his team continue to help families buy, sell and invest in real estate.

# Marc Sachnoff

A serial entrepreneur and twenty year entertainment industry veteran, Marc has produced, written or directed over 150 hours of broadcast television including "Sesame Street's 25th Anniversary," the 10 hour "History of Rock 'N Roll," the 1993 Presidential Inaugural and has received numerous awards including two prime time Emmy nominations for his work. Marc is also a 27 year practicing Buddhist who has made it his mission to bring the Buddha to business. He is now CEO/Chief Parent of The Parents Union – a Seattle based education reform non-profit.

# Kristen Marie Schuerlein

For nearly two decades, Kristen has been translating the ideas and inspirations of visionary leaders into brands and businesses. She is a serial entrepreneur who started her first company at age 26 providing graphic design and marketing strategy to home builders, tech start ups and entrepreneurs in a variety of industries. Today she co-owns a company whose mission is to deliver high-conscious digital content to a worldwide community of people dedicated to experiencing happiness and success in life.